Trucks

David and Penny Glover

First published in 2007 by Wayland

Copyright © Wayland 2007
This paperback edition published in 2010 by Wayland

Wayland
338 Euston Road
London NW1 3BH

Wayland
Level 17/207 Kent Street
Sydney, NSW 2000

Editor: Camilla Lloyd
Editorial Assistant: Katie Powell
Designer: Elaine Wilkinson
Picture Researcher: Diana Morris

Picture Acknowledgements: The author and publisher would like to thank the following for allowing these pictures to be reproduced in this publication: Cover: Christine Osbourne/Corbis, Eddie Stobart; Jacques Jangoux/ Alamy: 4, PB Galleries/Alamy: 22; Alan Schein/Corbis: 1, 6, Dave G. Houser/Corbis: 9t, Vince Streano/Corbis: 14b, Corbis: 11, 13t, 13c, 18, Patrick Bennett/Corbis: 12b, Helen King/Corbis: 14t, George Hall/Corbis: 15, Christine Osbourne/Corbis: 16, Lester Lefkowitz/Corbis: 17, Valentin A. Enrique/Sygma/Corbis: 19, Duomo/Corbis: 20, Bettmann/Corbis: 21; Juan Silva/Image Bank/Getty Images: 5, Walter Hodges/Stone/Getty Images: 7, 8, Mitch Kezar/Stone /Getty Images: 10; JCB: 12t; John Callan/Shout Picture Library: 9c.
With special thanks to JCB and Eddie Stobart.

British Library Cataloguing in Publication Data
Glover, David, 1953 Sept. 4-
        Trucks. - (On the go)
        1. Trucks - Juvenile literature
        I. Title II. Glover, Penny
        629.2'24

ISBN 978 07502 6155 5

Printed in China

Wayland is a division of Hachette Children's Books
www.hachette.co.uk

Contents

What are trucks?

Trucks are vehicles that carry **loads**. A big road truck may carry food, furniture or other things. This truck is carrying tree trunks.

load

A fork-lift truck moves loads in a factory. The driver slides the fork under the load, and then lifts it into place. This fork-lift truck is lifting and moving boxes.

box

fork

Truck quiz
What does a fork-lift truck do?

Truck parts

The front part of the truck is called the **tractor**. This is where the driver sits in the **cab**. The tractor has an **engine**. The tractor pulls the **trailer.**

cab

trailer

tractor

wheels

The trailer carries the load. It does not have an engine. Its wheels turn as the tractor pulls it.

This is an **articulated truck**.
It bends when it turns a corner.
The truck can have one or
more trailers.

Truck quiz
**Which part of a
truck has an engine?**

What is inside?

The driver turns the steering wheel to steer the truck. His cab is high up so he has a good view. The driver uses the gear stick to go at different speeds.

speedometer

steering wheel

gear stick

This trailer is called a **Winnebago**. It is a travelling home. Inside there are beds, cupboards, a kitchen and a bathroom. There is even a TV inside!

Truck quiz
What does the gear stick do?

What makes it go?

engine

The truck's engine makes it go.
It turns the wheels to pull the
truck along. The engine is in
the tractor underneath the cab.
The engine runs on **diesel fuel**.

The truck's wheels turn on **axles**. Axles are rods that fix the wheels to the truck's body. The wheels have thick rubber tyres to grip the road.

axle

wheel

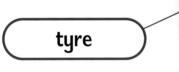

tyre

Truck quiz
What fuel does a truck engine use?

Dumper truck

A dumper truck is very tough. It carries soil and rocks. The trailer tips up to dump the load.

load

trailer

rubbish bin

Rubbish truck

A rubbish truck lifts and tips the bins. Then a **crusher** squashes the rubbish down.

12

Breakdown truck

A breakdown truck has a **winch**. The winch pulls the car onto the ramp.

ramp

winch

Truck quiz
Which truck has a crusher?
What does it do?

Special trucks

Double-decker truck

Some trucks are made to carry special loads or do special jobs. This **double-decker truck** carries cars.

top deck

bottom deck

drum

Cement mixer truck

It carries wet cement in its giant drum.

Ladder truck

Fire fighters use a ladder truck
to fight a fire in a tall building.
The hoses squirt water into the
flames to put out the fire.

hose

ladder

Truck quiz
What does a cement truck
carry in its drum?

Record breakers

Road trains are the longest trucks in the world. They travel on long, straight roads across Australia and America. This Road train has three trailers.

tractor

trailers

Giant dumper trucks
are the heaviest
trucks in the world.
They work in
quarries and mines.

This giant dumper
truck could carry
a whole house in
its huge trailer.
Its wheels are twice
as tall as a man.

Truck quiz
**Which countries have the
longest trucks in
the world?**

Driving safely

A truck driver must take care to drive safely. He must always wear a seatbelt and watch the road ahead. The driver checks his mirrors before **overtaking**. If there are no other vehicles coming, it is safe to pull out.

mirror

headlamps

flashing indicator lights

At night the truck's headlamps light up the road. The driver can see what's ahead. Other drivers can see the truck coming. Flashing indicator lights show that the truck is turning.

Truck quiz

How do you know if a truck is turning?

Truck fun

Trucks take part in competitions
and shows. A monster truck has
huge wheels on a small body.
It can drive over a pile of old cars.

flatbed trailer

A truck with a flatbed trailer makes a good carnival float. The carnival team decorate their float and dress in colourful costumes.

Truck quiz

What kind of truck trailer makes a good carnival float?

Old trucks

This truck is one hundred years old.
The first trucks were powered by
steam engines. The truck driver
puts coal onto a fire in the engine
to keep the truck going.

Truck words

articulated truck
A truck that bends between the tractor and trailer.

axle
The rod through the centre of a wheel.

cab
The part of the truck in which the driver sits.

crusher
The part of a rubbish truck that squashes the rubbish.

diesel
The fuel a truck engine uses to make it go.

double-decker truck
A truck with two levels for carrying loads. Car transporters are double-deckers.

engine
The part of the tractor that makes it move.

fuel
Something that burns inside an engine to make it work.

load
The things that the truck carries from place to place.

overtaking
When one vehicle goes past another on the road.

steam engine
An engine that works by using steam.

tractor
The front part of the truck that pulls the trailer.

trailer
The part of the truck that carries the load.

winch
A part that winds up a wire to pull up a load.

Winnebago
A trailer that can be used as a travelling home.

Quiz answers

Page 5 A fork-lift truck moves loads in factories.

Page 7 The tractor.

Page 9 It makes the truck go at different speeds.

Page 11 Diesel fuel.

Page 13 A rubbish truck. It squashes the rubbish down.

Page 15 Wet cement.

Page 17 Australia and America.

Page 19 Its indicator lights flash.

Page 21 A flatbed trailer.

Index